Prayers for the Journey

By
Audrey Jackson

This book of prayers is dedicated to:

My Lord and Savior, Jesus Christ, and to all
His saints who love to pray.

Special Dedication
To the memory of my granddaughter,
Alicia Monet Jackson
who tragically passed away December 2, 2010.

Her beautiful smile and
warm loving heart will never be forgotten.

Prayers for the Journey
Copyright © 2011 Audrey C. Jackson All Rights Reserved.

Acknowledgements

Special Thanks!

- To my husband Oswald, for his love and support.

- To my sons, Kevin, Kyle, and Kaylor, and their families who have experienced the power of these prayers.

- To my best friend Elder Barbara Manning, who edited my efforts and who offered encouragement to get these prayers published.

- To my pastor, Earl Harris, for believing in me and supporting me in this endeavour.

- To Melissa White, my friend, who prophesied to me in 2003 that I would write and publish books.

- To my artist friend, Mary Fusco, who provided the cover artwork and gave me suggestions for the title of this book.

- To my church family who loved and trusted me enough to pray my written prayers over the years.

Introduction

The prayers in this book were written over a period of time for the benefit of my church family. They were written in an effort to help us all grow in our prayer life and to draw us closer to our Creator.

Early on in my walk with the Lord, He taught me the importance of prayer in this journey. Because our spiritual journey takes many twists and turns, many different types of prayers were necessary to help us navigate the various storms that we encountered. Therefore, most of these prayers were birthed out of a specific need that I had, or a specific need for the church.

It is my desire that these prayers will help you begin a process that will lead you into a deeper relationship with our Lord and Savior. May they provide assistance to you in this incredible and wonderful journey experience of praying specific prayers that apply to specific needs.

Prayer is the key to the kingdom, faith unlocks the door.

Prayers for the Journey

Table of Contents

Dedication 2
Acknowledgements 3
Introduction 4

Scriptural Prayers

    Psalm 19 Prayer 9
    Psalm 23 Prayer 10
    Psalm 84 Prayer 11
    Psalm 91 Prayer 12
    Psalm 103 Prayer 13
    My Fortress 14
    The Joy of Forgiveness 15
    Intercession for Our Nation 16
    Live By the Spirit 17
    Praying the Scripture 18
    Jesus, Our Savior, Lord and King 19

Personal Prayers

    Renew My Mind 21
    Praise Prayer 22
    Consecrate Me to Your Service 23
    Controlling My Thoughts 24
    Praise and Thanksgiving 25
    Sinner's Prayer for Salvation 26
    Confession of My Sins 27
    Asking for Forgiveness of Sin 28
    My Identity in Christ 29
    Abuse of Food 30
    A Man's Prayer 31
    Healing Prayer 32

    Prayer of Faith 33
    Grace of God Prayer 34
    Prayer for A Mate 35
    Prayer Over Fear 36
    Give Unto the Lord 37
    Offense Prayers 38

Spiritual Warfare Prayers
    Stronghold of Rebellion 40
    Shattering My Strongholds 41
    Freedom from Addiction 42
    Freedom in Christ Prayer 43
    Protection for my Mind 44
    Prayer for Spiritual Cleansing of Home 45
    Prayer for Protection 46
    Letting Go of Bitterness 47
    Prayer to Break Generational Bondage 48
    Stronghold Prayer 49
    Prayer for Restoration 50

Prayers of Intercession
    A Prayer for Our Pastor 52
    A Prayer for Our Nation 53
    A Prayer for Our Children and Grandchildren 54
    A Prayer for the Harvest 56
    Confession of the Church 57
    House of Prayer 58
    A Prayer for Our Men 59
    Prayer for the Out Pouring of the Holy Spirit 60
    Prayer for Our Fathers 62
    Prayer for Racial Harmony 63

SCRIPTURAL PRAYERS

Psalm 19 Prayer

Lord God, the heavens declare the glory of you and the firmaments display and show your handiwork. Day after day the stars, the moon, and the sun, continue to speak, and night after night they reveal knowledge. They speak without a sound or a word, their voice is not heard. Yet, their message has gone out to all the earth, and their words to the entire world. The sun lives in the heavens where you have placed it; it rises from one end of heaven and follows its course to the other end. Nothing can hide from its heat.

Lord, your law is perfect, as it converts and revives my soul. Your precepts are right; rejoicing my heart. Your commandments are pure and bright; enlightening my eyes and giving me insight. The fear of you Lord is clean, pure and enduring forever. Your laws and ordinances are true and righteous. They are more desirable than honey, and in keeping and obeying them, there is great reward.

Cleanse me from hidden sins lurking in my heart. Keep me from deliberate sin. Don't let them control me. Let the words of my mouth, and the meditations of my heart, be pleasing and acceptable in your sight, O Lord, my rock and my redeemer.

Psalm 23 Prayer

I thank you Lord for being my Shepherd. Thank you for taking care of all my needs, as well as my wants. When I need rest, you provide a place for me to lie down in green soothing pastures. When I am thirsty and in need of a cool drink, you lead me to still peaceful waters.

My soul is refreshed and restored by you. When I wander off course, you gently step in and lead me in paths of righteousness, not because I deserve it, but for the sake of your name.

Even though I walk through the deep, dark valley of the shadow of death, I will fear no evil, because I know you are with me. I feel the presence of your protection as I am comforted by your rod and your staff.

Thank you Lord for preparing a table for me in the presence of my enemies. I will sit at the table knowing that you have called and anointed me to be here. Your anointing of oil on my head is so abundant, it is overflowing with blessings.

I am confident that your goodness, your mercy, and your unfailing love are always with me. They follow me every day of my life and I will dwell in your house and in your presence forever.   Amen.

Psalm 84 Prayer

How lovely is your dwelling place, O Lord of hosts! My soul longs and yearns to enter into your courts. My heart and my flesh cry out and sing for joy to you, because you are the living God.

Even the sparrows and the swallows have found a home and a nest for themselves where they can lay their young near your altar, O Lord of hosts, my king and my God. Blessed are those who dwell in your house and in your presence, they are always singing praises to you.

Lord, blessed are those whose strength is in you, those who set their minds on a pilgrim's journey to Mount Zion. As they pass through the dry valley, it becomes a place of springs; the early rain fills it. They grow stronger as they go.

O Lord, God of hosts, hear my prayer. Give me your ear. A day spent in your courts is better than a thousand anywhere else. Lord, I would rather be a doorkeeper in your house than to dwell in comfort in the tents of the wicked.

Lord God, you are my light and my protector. Thank you for giving me grace and glory. Thank you for not withholding good things from those who do what is right. O Lord of hosts, blessed is the one who trusts in you, who leans and depends on you. Hallelujah, Hallelujah, Hallelujah!

Psalm 91 Prayer

I thank you Lord that I dwell in the secret place of the Most High and I rest under the shadow and protection of you, the Almighty God. Lord, you are my refuge and my place of safety, in you I will trust. You save me from the snares of the enemy and from his deadly diseases. You cover me with your feathers and under your wings, I will find refuge. Your faithfulness is my shield and armor.

I will not fear terror by night nor the arrows that fly by day, nor the pestilence that stalks in the darkness, nor disaster that strikes at midday. A thousand may fall at my side and ten thousand at my right hand but it will not come near me. Because I make the Most High my dwelling place, no harm will happen to me and no disaster will come near me.

Thank you Lord, for you command your angels to guard and protect me in all my ways. They will lift me up to protect me from striking my foot against a stone. I will tread upon the lion and the cobra, and trample the great lion and the serpent under my feet.

Lord, you said that if I love you and truly know who you are, you will rescue me and keep me safe. When I am in trouble, I can call out to you and you will answer. You will be there to protect and honor me. I will live a long life and see your saving power.

Psalm 103 Prayer

Lord, I bless you with all my soul, all my inner most being praises your name. I do not forget your benefits; you forgive my sins and you heal my diseases. Lord, you keep me from the pit and bless me with love and mercy. You fill my life with good things so I stay young and strong like the eagle.

You are a merciful and loving God, slow to anger and abounding in love and mercy. You don't punish me as I deserve or repay me according to my sins and transgressions. As high as the heaven is above the earth, that is how great your love and mercy is toward those who fear and reverence you. As far as the east is from the west, that is how far you have removed my sins and transgressions from me.

Lord, you look upon your children who fear you with pity. You know what we are made of and you remember we are but dust. I thank you that your mercy is from everlasting to everlasting for those who honor and fear you. Your righteousness extends to the children' children, to all those who are true to your covenant, and who faithfully obey your commands.

Your throne, O God, is established in heaven and your kingdom rules over everything. All creation praises your name. Your strong and mighty angels who do your bidding and obey your word praise you. All your heavenly hosts who serve you and do your will praise you.

As for me — I also praise you. Bless the Lord, O my soul.

My Fortress
Based on Psalm 31

O Lord, I come to you for protection. You are my rock and my fortress. Hear my cry for help; I need to be rescued quickly. Be for me a great rock of safety, a fortress where my enemies cannot reach me.

For the honor of your name, lead me out of this peril. Pull me out of this trap my enemies have secretly set for me, for I find protection in you alone. Rescue me for you are a faithful God.

Let your favor shine on me, O Lord, don't let me be disgraced. Don't let me be put to shame. Let the wicked be disgraced. Let their lying lips, those proud and arrogant lips that accuse the godly, be put to silence.

Lord, I am overcome with joy because of your unfailing love. You have seen my troubles, and you care about the anguish of my soul. You have not handed me over to my enemy but have set me in a safe place. I trust in you, O Lord, for you are my God. My future is in your hands.

Oh how great is your goodness which you have stored up for those who fear and honor you. Thank you for hiding me in the secret place of your presence; safe from those who conspire against me, and far from accusing lips.

I praise you Lord for you have shown me your marvelous kindness and unfailing love.

The Joy of Forgiveness
Based on Psalm 32:1-5

Thank you Lord that, you bless those whose transgressions are forgiven, and whose sins are covered. Thank you that you bless those in whom you did not impute iniquity; whose sin you did not count against them. Thank you that you bless those in whose spirit there is no deceitfulness, no guile.

Lord, when I kept silent about my sin; when I refused to confess to you, my bones wasted away. I was weak and miserable, and I groaned all day long. For long periods of time, your hand of displeasure was heavy upon me. My strength was sapped as in the heat of summer.

When I finally came to my senses and acknowledged my sin to you; and did not try any longer to hide or cover up my iniquity. When I said I will confess my transgressions to you Lord, you forgave the iniquity of my sin, and you lifted the guilt from me. The pressure and the burden were gone. Thank you Lord, you are indeed a forgiving and loving God.

Intercession for Our Nation
Based on Daniel 9

O Lord, you are a great and awesome God. You always fulfill your covenant of love and mercy to those who love you and keep your commandments. We as a nation have sinned and done wrong in your sight. We have rebelled against you and scorned your commands and ordinances. We have refused to listen to your servants who are speaking on your behalf.

Lord, you are righteous, but we and our ancestors are covered with shame. We have not followed your laws and decrees. We have become a disgrace to you because of our unfaithfulness.

O Lord God, in view of your righteousness, we pray that you turn away all your anger and wrath from our cities and our nation. Hear our prayers and partitions. For your own sake, Lord, smile again on this nation.

Give ear, O God, and hear our request. O Lord, we ask that you hear our cry, and forgive us of our wickedness. We do not make this request because we deserve it; we make it because of your great mercy.

Live By the Spirit
Galatians 5:16-21

Lord, you have told us in your word to live and walk in the Holy Spirit so we would not fulfill the lust of the flesh. As I read your word, I understand better the struggle that is taking place in me, and the need to rely upon your Spirit to lead and guide me in my walk.

The old nature loves and wants to do sinful things, while the Holy Spirit gives me desires that are opposite to what the sinful nature wants. When I go off on my own, I give in to the desires of my flesh even when I don't want to. Evidences of this are: my eagerness for lustful pleasure, selfish ambition, outburst of anger, rebellion, impure thoughts, sexual immorality, idolatry, greed, drunkenness, envy and jealousy.

Lord, I need more of your Holy Spirit. Your word said you would give me more of the Holy Spirit if I ask (Luke 11:13). I ask you now to fill me with the power of your Spirit. Help me to follow after, and be led by your Spirit. Give me grace to see I cannot do this on my own. I need your power.

Help me to be holy as you are holy. Help me to see that I must daily read your word, I must daily be in prayer to you, I must continue to be a disciple, I must deny myself, and I must consciously seek after you and live the life you called me to live. This I pray in the name of your son, Jesus. Amen.

Praying the Scripture
Ephesians 3:14-21

Father God, I bow my knees to you, the Father of our Lord Jesus Christ, from whom the whole family in earth is named. I pray that out of Your glorious riches You may strengthen me with power through Your Holy Spirit in my inner being, so that Christ may dwell in my heart through faith.

I pray to be rooted and grounded in love, and understand, along with all the saints, how wide, and long, and high and deep is the love of Jesus Christ. I want to know this love that surpasses knowledge and to be filled with all the fullness of God.

Now to You who is able to do exceedingly, abundantly above all that I ask or think, according to Your power that is at work within me. To You be all the glory. Amen.

Jesus, Our Savior, Lord And King

He who is the blessed and only Potentate, the King of kings, and Lord of lords, who alone has immortality, dwelling in unapproachable light, whom no man has seen or can see, to whom be honor and everlasting power. Amen. *(1Timothy 6:15-16)*

To Him who is able to keep you from falling and to present you before His glorious presence without fault and with great joy — to the only God our Savior, be glory, majesty, power and authority, through Jesus Christ our Lord, before all ages, now and forever more! Amen. *(Jude 1:24-25)*

Now to the King eternal, immortal, invisible, the only wise God, be honor and glory forever and ever. Amen. *(1Timothy 1:17)*

PERSONAL PRAYERS

Renew My Mind

Father God, I thank you for my mind, that part of me that can think, reason, learn, comprehend, plan, imagine, and dream.

Your Word tells me in Romans 12:2 to renew my mind so I will know your good and perfect will. Lord, I truly want to know your will so I can follow you. I no longer want my mind set on things of this world that appeal to my flesh. I no longer want my thoughts to be self-centered. I don't want to continue learning things from a worldly view and a limited perspective.

Strengthen me Lord, to do what is necessary to clean out my mind. Help me to put aside those things that pollute my mind and affect me negatively. Motivate me to study and meditate on your Word, so I can recognize wrong thinking. Give me strength to resist lying thoughts. Set my mind on things above, heavenly things. Help me to realize that I am now seated with Christ and my mind needs to look at things from a heavenly perspective.

When the enemy tries to attack my mind with impure and untrue thoughts and vain imaginations, prompt me to take them captive to the obedience of Christ as your Word states. Enable me to be strong in you Lord, and in the power of your might. Help me to be anxious for nothing, but in everything by prayer and supplication, with thanksgiving, let my request be made known to you.

Finally Lord, help me to think only on those things that are true, just, honest, pure, lovely, and are of a good report. In the name of Jesus I pray. Amen.

Praise Prayer

Lord God, you are great and greatly to be praised. Your greatness is unsearchable. You are high and lifted up and worthy to be praised. You are my creator, my life-giver, my redeemer, my healer, my deliverer, the One who sits enthroned in heaven.

I praise you for your mighty acts and your wonderful works. I praise you because you are a merciful God, slow to anger and abounding in love. I praise you because you are a forgiving God, forgiving me of my sins and cleansing me from all unrighteousness.

You are the King of kings and the Lord of lords, and your kingdom is forever. I magnify and glorify your name for you alone are holy. Blessings and honor and glory and power are to you who sits on the throne, and to the Lamb, forever and ever. You are worthy, O Lord, to receive glory and honor and power, for you created all things, and by your will they exist.

> I praise you with an upright heart;
> I praise you as I lift up my hands:
> I praise you with my lips;
> I praise you with the dance;
> I praise you with instruments;

For you are the King eternal, immortal, invisible, the only wise God. Be glory and majesty, dominion and power, both now and forever. Amen.

Consecrate Me to Your Service

Father God, your word tells me to submit my body to you as a living sacrifice, holy, and acceptable, this is my reasonable service, my spiritual act of worship. Lord, convict me to obey you in this command. Help me to understand the depth of what you have done for me. Open my heart to the knowledge that you gave me mercy when I was dead in my trespasses and sins, so in view of this mercy, I owe you my body to be used as your instrument.

Please forgive me for thinking my body belongs to me and that I can do anything I want with it. Let me not forget all that Jesus endured when He went to the Cross for me. Remind me of the price He paid to redeem me back to you. Help me realize that my body is the temple of the Holy Spirit and I am to glorify you in my body and in my spirit. Give me clean hands and a pure heart. Open my eyes to see you in the beauty of holiness. Let my ears hear your truth and not the lies of the enemy. Keep my feet in the path of righteousness.

Lord, I give myself to you right now to be used as your vessel. Consecrate me to your service. Strengthen me to seek after godliness and holiness and not to be conformed any longer to this world. Bless me so I can be a blessing to others. In the name of Jesus, I pray. Amen.

Controlling My Thoughts

Heavenly Father, I submit myself to you with all my weaknesses, especially in the area of my thoughts. You know my thoughts and are acquainted with all my ways. Make me a clean vessel fit for your use.

Lord, please forgive me of my impure and improper thoughts. I confess that I have not done what is needed to renew my mind. Convict me to use your Word as a weapon to fight these unholy and vain thoughts. Your Word is alive and more powerful than any weapon known to man. It has the power to pull down all evil strongholds.

Father, give me a clean heart and renew a right spirit in me. Remind me to not engage in damaging talk about myself or others, but rather to dwell on good attributes. Help me to take all negative and unholy thoughts captive to the obedience of Christ.

Thank you for giving me the helmet of salvation to guard my mind. Thank you for giving me the mind of Christ. Help me to realize that I can think like Christ if I think on things that are pure, lovely, and of a good report.

I am what I think in my heart so I will think on things that are spiritually uplifting and edifying. Thank you for the victory. In the name of Jesus I pray. Amen.

Praise and Thanksgiving

Lord, I enter into your gates with thanksgiving and into your courts with praise. I praise you for who you are; my creator, my sustainer, my provider. You are a good God, merciful, kind and loving. I acknowledge your holiness and bow down in humble adoration at your throne. You are Lord of lords and King of kings!

I will bless your name, and your praise shall continually be in my mouth. My soul shall boast of you. You are high and exalted; there is no one like you. I praise you for your mighty acts; I praise you for your excellent greatness. How excellent is your name in all the earth!

Father, thank you for loving me enough to, send Jesus to save me. Thank you for your Holy Spirit, who fills me, comforts me, guides me and teaches me your truth. You are Jehovah-Jireh, my provider, who meets my every need. Thank you for your Word which is a lamp to guide me and a light for my path.

Thank you for forgiving all my sins and for healing all my diseases. Thank you for restoring my soul, and for keeping me in the paths of righteousness for your name's sake. I will praise you in everything, my Lord and my Redeemer. In the mighty name of Jesus Christ, I pray. Amen.

Sinner's Prayer for Salvation

Lord Jesus Christ, I know you love me because you died on the cross for my sins. I confess that I am a sinner and cannot save myself. I believe that you are the Son of God and that you died, and was raised from the dead and now sit at the right hand of the Father. I do now by faith gladly accept you as my Savior, Lord, and Master. Thank you, Lord Jesus for my eternal salvation.

(The above prayer must be spoken out loud)

If you prayed this prayer (confessed with your mouth) and believe in your heart that Jesus came and died for you, you are saved!
Romans 10:9-10

Now join a good Bible teaching Church, read your Bible, pray to God, and become a disciple (learner) of Jesus Christ.

Confession of My Sins

O God, I ask that you search me, and test my heart. Point out anything in me that offends you, and lead me along the path of everlasting life. I confess that I have sinned and done things that are evil in your sight. Have mercy on me and blot out my sins.

Give me a clean heart, O God, and renew a right spirit in me. I know you desire truth and honesty in my heart so you can teach me your ways. Purify my thoughts — wash me with hyssop and I shall be clean. Restrain me from willful sins, and forgive my hidden faults. Keep me on the path of righteousness for your name's sake.

May the words that come from my mouth, and may the things that I think and meditate on, be pleasing and acceptable in your sight. May the songs that I sing to you be a sweet, sweet, sound in your ears. May your ears be open and attentive to my prayers.

Father, I thank you for your forgiveness, and I thank you for lifting the burden of my sins. I am grateful that you are a merciful, loving, and forgiving God. In Jesus' name I pray. Amen.

Psalms 19:12-14; 23:3; 51:1, 6-7, 10; 139:23-24

My Identity in Christ

Lord God, I pray that I will always find my identity in you. When I am feeling inadequate and downcast, help me to understand my worth through your eyes and by your standards. May I recognize the unique qualities you have placed in me and be able to appreciate them.

Your Word says I am fearfully and wonderfully made. You made all my delicate, inner parts and knit me together in my mother's womb. You said that I am your workmanship, created in Christ Jesus for good works, which you prepared beforehand for me to do. Open my eyes to see myself the way you see me. Enable me to love and appreciate myself. Help me to understand and receive this amazing love you have for me.

Lord God, I thank you for my life. I thank you that you love me and chose me in Christ before the foundation of the world; and that you have accepted me in your kingdom. I pray right now to receive this love you have for me, and to experience your peace and your joy in my heart. In Jesus' name I pray. Amen.

Abuse of Food

Father, I thank you for the body that you created and gave to me. It is a wonderful vessel and I am grateful that you formed it just for my use. I pray that my body, soul and spirit are in harmony with your will for me. Help me not to abuse my body by over indulgence of food. Lord, I confess there are times when I use food to comfort me, and to satisfy my emotional needs. Help me to recognize hunger as the reason to consume food, and not my emotional needs.

Forgive me for using food to medicate myself when the pain of unhealed hurts seems too much. I confess that I have been eating to excess, as well as consuming foods that are damaging my health. Forgive me for doing this and help me to return to eating for nourishment, and energy only. I pray that you will fortify me to break loose from the bad eating habits I have acquired. Teach me listen to my body and not be governed by unmet needs of my soul. When I feel an emotional need arising in me, help me seek your Word and feast on it, drawing close to you in prayer and meditation.

Lord, I know you are able to heal wounds, and to fill the void in my life with your love and grace. I ask you now for strength to overcome the strong desire to overindulge my body with food. Place in me a stronger desire to obey you and to take care of my body. In the name of Jesus I pray. Amen.

Asking for Forgiveness of Sin

Lord God, I am sorry that I have sinned against you. I come humbly to you confessing my sin of _____, asking you to forgive me. Your word said that if I confess my sin, You are faithful and just to forgive me. You are a loving God, full of mercy and compassion. You are a Holy God, hating sin but loving the sinner.

Lord, I repent of my sin, and with your help I will make the necessary changes in my life so I do not repeat this sin. Give me the desire to read your Word when I am tempted to yield to sin. Create in me a clean heart and renew a right spirit in me. Free me from negative and impure thoughts. Help me to renew my mind by thinking on good, pure, and beautiful things.

You desire truth in my inner being, so make me to know wisdom in my inmost heart. Help me to recognize my own faults and shortcomings and not to blame others for my sins. O Lord, give me a broken and a contrite heart, this You do not despise.

Thank you for your forgiveness. Thank you for removing the weight of my sin and lifting the burden of my guilt. Thank you for forgetting my sin and removing it as far as the east is from the west. In Jesus' name I pray. Amen.

A Man's Prayer

Heavenly Father, I commit myself to your will, and acknowledge you as Lord of my life. Thank you for saving me and giving me the gift of your Holy Spirit for that day of redemption.

Lord, forgive me for relinquishing my rightful place in your kingdom, and for not always fulfilling my role as son, husband, father, brother, friend. Forgive me for my lack of courage when I had opportunity to pray, or say a word for you publicly, but didn't. Forgive me for my misplaced, and sometimes uncontrolled, out-bursts of anger.

Forgive me for hanging on to my sinful pride especially when it caused me to hold a grudge rather than forgive; to be combative rather then submit; to dominate rather than love; to argue and talk rather than listen. Forgive me for the times I have been envious and jealous when someone else received something I wanted. Forgive me for my lustful thoughts and desires. Forgive me for lying and living in denial about my true condition. Forgive me for rebelling against you when I refused to believe and obey the word from your messenger.

Father, I pray that you will deliver me from the evil spirits of pride, rebellion, fear, anger, jealousy, lying, lust, and rejection. Shatter all my strongholds and strengthen me to overcome the snares of the devil. Lord, change my heart and make it pure. Give me a thankful heart and a praying spirit. Fill me with your Holy Spirit so I will be bolder in my service for you. Put praise for you in my mouth, in my hands, and in my feet. Restore to me the joy of my salvation. In Jesus' name, I pray. Amen.

Healing Prayer

Father God, I come to your throne boldly in faith to receive my healing. I confess your Word, believing that your Word will not return to you void, but will accomplish what it says it will. Thank you Jesus that you borne my sickness and carried my sorrow and pain.

I have confidence in the Word which abides in me to heal me. I have on the whole armor of God, and the shield of faith protects me from the fiery darts of the wicked one. Lord, I reverence and worship you, and ask that your angels encamp round about me and deliver me from every evil work of the enemy.

In the name of Jesus, I bind every spirit of afflictions and infirmities from operating against me in any way. I am the property of God Almighty, and I give no place in me to the enemy. I remain stable and fixed under the shadow of the Almighty, whose power no foe can withstand.

Father, your Word says that my tongue has the power of life and death; therefore, I speak words filled with faith, hope, life, and health. I declare that I have a sound mind and wholeness of body and spirit from the deepest parts of my nature in my immortal spirit even to the joints and marrow of my bones.

I believe that healing is the children' bread, and as your child, I receive total and complete healing for my body, soul, and spirit. Your Word is health, life, and medicine to me, and I refuse to tolerate any symptoms of sickness or disease. Because of the stripes on your back, I believe that I am healed. I thank you, and I praise you. In Jesus' name, I pray. Amen.

Prayer of Faith

Lord God, I pray that you will increase my faith and enlarge my ability to believe in you, your Word, your promises, your ways, and your power. Put a longing in me to talk to you and hear your voice. Give me an understanding of what it means to soak in your presence, acknowledging you in everything I do.

Lord, you said that "faith comes by hearing and hearing by the Word of God" (Romans 10:17). Convict me to feed my spirit with your Word so my faith grows big enough to believe that with you all things are possible. Give me an unfailing certainty that what you promise to do, you will do. Give me the courage to take a leap of faith today, realizing that my faith is my shield of protection as I pray to move the mountain in my life.

Your Word says "the just shall live by faith" (Romans 1:17), so I pray to live the type of faith-filled life you called us all to undergo. May my journey be a step-by-step process of walking with you by faith, being led and guided by your Holy Spirit. Increase my knowledge of you and your promises for your church. Remove any doubt and unbelief from my mind.

Lord, I want to trust in you with all my heart and not to lean on my own understanding. May I always put my trust in you, even when I don't understand how you are working things out. Help me to walk by faith, and not by sight. I thank you and I praise you.

In the name of Jesus, I pray. Amen.

Grace of God Prayer

Thank you Spirit of Grace that you love me so much you sent your son, Jesus Christ to die for my sins. When I think of the kind of love you demonstrated in reconciling fallen man back to you, I cannot but weep for joy. You are indeed an awesome God who is worthy of all praise.

The Word says that all have sinned and fallen short of your glory, but your grace (unmerited favor) was extended to all who believe in your Son. I thank you Lord for wooing and drawing me to Jesus, and for opening my eyes to see that I needed a Savior.

I thank you Jesus for becoming flesh and dwelling among us, full of grace and truth. Help me to walk worthy of your calling. Grant me, according to the riches of your glory, to be strengthened with might in my inner being. Remind me that I can come to your throne of grace to receive help in times of need.

Lord, I ask that you keep me humble, for your Word says you resist the proud, but you give grace to the humble. May I be strengthened with grace that will enable me to live the kind of life that is pleasing to you. Fill me with the knowledge of your will in all wisdom and spiritual understanding.

In the name of Jesus, I pray. Amen.

Prayer for a Mate

Lord God, I love you and I thank you for being my Lord and Savior, my Healer, my Deliverer, my Counselor and my Comforter.

Father, I pray that you will send me someone to love and to share my life with. Purify my motives for a relationship with a partner. Help me not to seek someone just to meet my unmet needs. Help me to understand that no person could ever fulfill such unrealistic expectations.

Lord Jesus, I know that you are the only one that can meet all of my needs. Please forgive me for the times I have blamed you for my loneliness and for my not having someone who cares just for me. Jesus, if there is a special person you have chosen and are preparing just for me, I ask that you draw them into a strong, whole relationship with you. Teach them to see you as the focus of their life, just as I am asking you to do with me.

Lord, help me to wait on your timing. Help me not to seek any such person through my own efforts. I put this request into your hands because you know what is best for me. You are the one that can do exceedingly abundantly above all that I ask or think. In Jesus' name I pray. Amen.

Prayer over Fear

Father God, I come to your throne in the mighty name of Jesus. Your Word said I should be anxious for nothing, but in everything by prayer and supplication with thanksgiving make my request be made known to you.

I bring all my worries and concerns to you and ask you to take away my irrational fears. I know that you have not given me a spirit of fear, but of love, power and a sound mind. Guard my mind from the attacks of the enemy. Deliver me from fear that destroys and replace it with godly fear.

Help me to realize that Jesus has set me free, and who the Son sets free is free indeed. Lord, you are my protection and even though I walk through the valley of the shadow of death, I will fear no evil for you are with me. Your goodness and your mercy follow me wherever I go. You are my helper in times of trouble; how great you are.

I declare that no weapon formed against me will prosper. I am an over comer and will walk in a spirit of power and strength, for you are my strength and my refuge, in you will I trust. I will not be afraid of the terror by night, nor of the arrow that flies by day, for you have given me your angels to guard me.

I thank you Lord for your love, power and a sound mind. Thank you for freeing me from the spirit of fear. I praise you for you are a loving and merciful God. In the name of Jesus, I pray. Amen.

Give Unto the Lord

Lord, you are great and greatly to be praised! You made the heavens and the earth and everything in them, they all belong to you. Honor and majesty are before you, strength and beauty are in your sanctuary.

I worship you in the beauty of holiness. I come before your presence to give you the glory due your name. Your Word says to bring you an offering as I come into your courts (Psalms 96:8). Dear Lord, please receive my offering as I give it cheerfully and with thanksgiving in our hearts.

All that I have belongs to you, so I willingly and joyfully return back to you a portion of what you have given me. I am truly grateful for the blessings you have given me, so much so that my cup is overflowing.

I thank you Father God for loving me so much that you gave your only Son to redeem me back to you. And when your Son went back to heaven, you sent the gift of your Holy Spirit. When I think of the precious gifts you gave, how could I not give back to you?

I bless your holy name as I bring my tithes and offerings to the Church house to help support kingdom building. Please use it for your glory. In the name of Jesus, I pray. Amen

When I Have Been Offended

Lord God, the Word says that you are my comforter and right now I need to be comforted. I am hurt and offended by what was said and what was done to me. Please take away the sting of the hurt and help me to release the offense. Help me to understand what may be going on in my offender's life that would cause them to do what they did to me. Take away from me any feelings of revenge toward this person. Fill me with your love and your mercy so I can bless them. I choose not to hold on to my resentment. Heal my damaged emotions and set me free from the bondage of bitterness. I choose to forgive and I now ask you to bless those who have hurt me. In Jesus' name I pray. Amen.

Not to Receive an Offense

Lord, forgive me for being offended because things did not go the way I wanted them to. Help me to relinquish control and learn to trust in you as well as others. Take away the pride and selfishness from my life. Purify my heart and take away all confidence in my flesh. Let love abound in me so that I am not easily offended. In Jesus' name I pray. Amen.

Not to Bring Offense

Lord, I ask that you fill me with your love and mercy so that I do not knowingly offend my sisters and brothers in Christ. Show me anything in my life that may be a stumbling block to others and remove it. If I should offend someone, help me to quickly seek forgiveness from the person I offended, as well as to seek your forgiveness. Amen.

SPIRITUAL WARFARE PRAYERS

Stronghold of Rebellion

Father, I come to you in the name of Jesus thanking you for your Word and your Holy Spirit who has made me aware of my sin of rebellion. Forgive me of any past or current involvement in rebellious acts against you and the people you have placed in authority. I love you Lord, and I want to live a life that is pleasing to you.

In the name of Jesus Christ, I bind the spirit of rebellion and stubbornness, and I loose the spirit of submission in my life. Any agreement or unholy bond made by me or my family, I declare to be broken right now. I renounce my participation in rebellion and stubbornness and ask the Holy Spirit to restore and fill me with your power.

Thank you Lord for freeing me from the stronghold of rebellion and. Thank you for giving me a spirit of submission. Thank you for your Word which states in Matthew 18:18 that whatever I bind and loosed on earth, will be bound and loosed in heaven. Amen.

Shattering My Strongholds

In the name of Jesus Christ, I bind the strongman and I loose his hold on everything he has stolen from me. I rebuke his work, and loose the power and effects of every deception, device, and influence he wants to bring against me.

Lord, I repent of having wrong attitudes, thoughts, ideas, desires, and beliefs. I renounce them now and ask your forgiveness. Father, forgive me as I forgive those who have caused me pain, loss, or grief. Take away from me any desire for retribution or redress.

In the name of Jesus, I loose all generational bondages and their strongholds from myself. Help me to overcome the effects of any harsh words or curses spoken about me, to me, or by me. I loose wrong patterns of thinking, and any bad habits or behaviors that may still be working in me.

Strengthen me, Lord, so that my behavior and spiritual desires will line up with the fruit of the Holy Spirit. Thank you, Jesus, that you have promised whatsoever I bind and loose on earth will be bound and loosed in heaven. Amen.

Freedom from Addiction

Father, I come to your throne of mercy seeking your face and your help in being delivered from this addiction. I believe that you are the all-powerful God and nothing is impossible for you.

Lord, I desire to be free from this bondage of (alcohol, drugs, tobacco, sex, pornography,) but I can't do it myself. I confess that I was weak and allowed the enemy to seduce me into this filthy addiction. I believe that you are a strong deliverer and that your Word which is truth can set me free. I surrender myself to you to be cleansed and purified. Remove from me this unhealthy and self-destructing craving. Protect me from the evil one who seeks to destroy me.

Give me the strength to live a life of purity. Help me stay away from places and people who are indulging in this type of lifestyle. Place people in my life that can give me godly counsel and will provide good fellowship. Convict me to renew my mind by reading and meditating on your Word. Help me to not yield to temptation but to be strong in the power of Jesus Christ.

I thank you Lord for freeing me from this addiction. Thank you for your love and your mercy. I praise you for you are worthy of all praise! In the name of Jesus I pray. Amen.

Freedom in Christ Prayer

Heavenly Father, I confess there are areas in my life that I have not yet surrendered to my Lord and Savior, Jesus Christ. Lord, please forgive me and cleanse me of all unrighteousness. Give me courage to face the truth and then to begin to pull down these strongholds without reluctance or willful deception in my heart. I submit all my inner most being to the light of the Holy Spirit of Truth to expose the strongholds of sin within me.

By the power of the Holy Spirit and in the name of Jesus Christ, I bind the satanic spirits that are influencing me to sin, and I loose the power and effect of their work. I proclaim that each stronghold in my life is coming down! Unforgiveness is coming down, fear is coming down, control and manipulation is coming down, self-indulgence is coming down, distrust is coming down, false pride is coming down, and anger is coming down!

I thank you Lord for forgiving and cleansing me. Thank you for your warfare weapons of prayer, of praise, of fasting, of the Word, of the Blood, and the mighty name of Jesus. Your weapons of warfare are indeed mighty in God for the pulling down of strongholds.

Blessed be the name of the Lord, for you are my Savior, my Healer and my Deliverer. Amen, amen, and amen.

Protection for My Mind

Lord God, I pray for protection for my mind. Shield me from the lies of the enemy. Help me to clearly discern between your voice and the voice of the enemy, and show me how to take every thought captive as you have instructed us to do *(2 Corinthians 10:5)*. Give me a thirst for your Word and a hunger for your truth so that I can recognize wrong thinking. Give me strength to resist lying thoughts. Remind me that I have the mind of Christ. Where the enemy's lies have already invaded my thoughts, I invite the power of the Holy Spirit to cleanse my mind.

Lord, you have given me authority over all the power of the enemy *(Luke 10:19)*. By that authority given to me in Christ Jesus, I command all lying spirits away from my mind. I proclaim that God has given me a sound mind. I will not entertain confusion, but live in clarity. I will not be tormented by impure, evil, negative, or sinful thoughts.

Enable me to be strong in you and in the power of your might *(Ephesians 6:10)*. Help me to be anxious for nothing, but in everything by prayer and supplication, with thanksgiving, let my request be made known to you, and may your peace, which surpasses all understanding, guard my heart and mind through Christ Jesus *(Philippians 4:6-7)*. And finally, whatever things are true, noble, honorable, pure, lovely, of a good report, or anything praise-worthy, let me think on these things *(Philippians 4:8)*.

Lord, thank you for your protection and the love that you have for me. Thank you for watching over me and allowing me to have a restful sleep. In Jesus name, I pray. Amen.

Prayer for Spiritual Cleansing of Home

Heavenly Father, I acknowledge that you are the Lord of heaven and earth. Thank You that you have brought me into your family and have blessed me with spiritual blessings in the heavenly places in Christ Jesus.

Thank you for this place where I live. I claim my home as a place of spiritual safety for me and my family and I ask for your protection from all the attacks of the enemy. You are my refuge and my fortress, in you will I trust.

In the mighty name of Jesus, I command every evil spirit claiming ground in this place, based on activities of past or present occupants, including me and my family, to leave now and never return. I renounce and break all demonic assignments directed against this home, and I apply the blood of Jesus over this home and all its possessions.

Lord, I ask that you post your holy angels around this home to guard it from any and all attempts of the enemy to reenter and interrupt your purposes for me and my family.

I thank you Lord for your divine protection and for your grace and blessings that you are showering on this family. In the name of Jesus, I pray. Amen.

Prayer for Protection

Lord God, I pray for your divine protection from all the schemes of the evil one. Keep me safe from all hurt, harm, and dangers that may be lurking in my path. Be my shield, my fortress, and my strong tower.

Thank you that I dwell in the secret place of the Most High, and under the shadow of your wings I will find refuge. Command your angels to guard me in all my ways. Save me from any plans of the enemy that seeks to destroy my life.

Watch over me and guide my every move. Alert me to any snares or traps that the enemy is setting for me. I pray and believe that even though bad things may be happening all around me, they will not come near me, for you are my God and I dwell with you.

In the name of Jesus, I pray. Amen.

Letting Go of Bitterness

Father, the pain of rejection is almost more than I can bear. Sometimes life seems so unjust, so unfair. The wounds of my past have left a residue of anger, outrage, rejection, and separation toward those who have hurt me. Take away from me any desire to avenge myself or to see something bad happen to my offender(s).

In the name of Jesus, I choose to forgive those who have wronged me. I do this because I recognize that you have forgiven me, so I too must walk in forgiveness. Help me Holy Spirit to get rid of all bitterness, anger, outrage and resentment. I pray for You to bless my offender(s) and to touch their lives with your mercy.

I know you are the One who destroys every yoke of bondage and binds up the brokenhearted. By faith, I receive your anointing and I receive your emotional healing. Thank you for giving me grace to stand firm until the process is completed.

I declare that I have overcome resentment and bitterness by the blood of Jesus and by the Word of my testimony. I thank you Father, for setting me free. I pray this prayer in Jesus' name. Amen.

Prayer to Break Generational Bondage

Father God, I come to you in the name and power of your son, Jesus Christ. I repent of my sins and the sins of my fathers that allowed these bondages in our family. Please forgive us for opening the door to the enemy and becoming enslaved to him.

I am grateful that the blood of Jesus has power to demolish all strongholds and bondages from me. So in the name of Jesus, I renounce every sin and every spirit that accompanies that sin, and I break the hold that sin had on me and my family members.

I plead and apply the blood of Jesus over my mind, spirit and my body. I break every yoke and bondage from my past and the past of my ancestors, and I sever those ties through the power of the blood of Jesus.

I declare that I and my children (and my children' children) are now free from the enemy's grip. Everything that the enemy has stolen will be restored to me. I am healed and set free in Jesus' name.

Lord, I thank you for the victory and I ask that you fill me with your love, your peace and your joy. In Jesus' name, I pray. Amen

Stronghold Prayer

Lord God, I pray that your will and purpose for my life be fulfilled in the manner in which you planned it. Teach me your truth so I will not be deceived by the subtle deceptions of the world and the devil. Align my mind to the mind of Christ so I will think like Him.

Lord, I repent of every ***wrong*** and ***ungodly*** desire, attitude, and pattern of thinking. Forgive me for holding onto these behaviors and habits. I renounce and reject them. I am standing on the truth of your Word that says whatever I bind and loose on earth has been bound and loosed in heaven.

In the name of Jesus, I bind the strongman and loose and reclaim every bit of joy, peace, blessings, material and spiritual possession he has stolen from me. I reject the enemy's influence over every part of my body, soul, and spirit. In the name of Jesus, I renounce every ***wrong*** and ***ungodly*** attitude, way of thinking, belief, and behavior that I have learned.

I break the power and effect of harsh words or curses spoken about me, to me, or by me. I break generational curses, and sicknesses of _____ that have occurred in my family. They have no more effect upon me or any member of my family. I bind and loose these strongholds in the name of Jesus Christ who has given me the keys and authority to do so. Amen.

Prayer for Restoration

Heavenly Father, thank you that our Lord Jesus disarmed the evil powers and authorities at the cross, and in His resurrection and glorification, made a spectacle of them (Colossians 2:15).

Lead us to remove the "high places" that the enemy gains in our lives through our personal and corporate disobedience and deception. Reveal to us our corporate sins so that we may renounce, repent, and reject them. Flood us with biblical truth that cleanses us from our sins. Forgive our lack of faith and trust in you. Forgive our lack of time in prayer to you. Forgive our disbelief and low expectation of how you answer prayer. Rid us from complacency and from being lukewarm.

Cleanse us of our unwillingness to forgive one another. Forgive our withholding sacrificial love and giving only what cost us nothing. We now forgive one another from our hearts for the times we have neglected, betrayed, retreated, hurt, damaged, misunderstood, deceived, or lied to one another.

Heal the pain and damage caused by the attacks of satan on our churches and leaders. Open our eyes to see any of the enemy's strongholds, and prompt us to use the sword of the Spirit to stand against them. Release your angels to accomplish for us and for our church everything you sent them to do.

Lord, fill us afresh and anew with the fullness of the Holy Spirit. We want to live in Him, walk with Him and keep in step with Him. We pray this prayer in the name of your son, Jesus Christ. Amen.

PRAYERS OF INTERCESSION

A Prayer for Our Pastor

Father God, your Word says that you give us shepherds according to your heart, pastors who will feed us with knowledge and understanding *(Jeremiah 3:15)*. We thank you for our pastor and we receive him as a gift from you *(Ephesians 4:11)*. We ask you to give our pastor a heart for the people in the congregation. Inspire him how to instruct and prepare us so we can do the work of the ministry.

Lord, give him a heart of compassion for those who are lost, that we may all effectively reach out to our community. Thank you for giving him the freedom to speak and boldly proclaim what you have placed in his heart. Grant him a fresh anointing of your wisdom and understanding, of your counsel and power, and of your knowledge. Continue to strengthen and encourage him in the ministry in which he has been called.

Bless him that he may always walk in your love. Help him to understand your will in order to live a life worthy of the gospel with purity and holiness. Protect him and his family from all harm. We pray and believe that no weapon formed against him will prosper, and any tongue that rises against him in judgment will be proven wrong.

Thank you Lord that you have given us the desire to stand behind our pastor and under gird him in prayer. Help us to say and speak only those things that will edify him. We ask your blessings for him right now in the name of Jesus Christ. Amen.

A Prayer for Our Nation

Heavenly Father, God of the universe, you are the only wise, omniscient, omnipotent, and omnipresent God. We acknowledge you as King of kings and Lord of lords. You are the creator of heaven and earth. All things were made by you and for you.

Lord, you made our nation and it was founded on our trust in you. We thank you for blessing us to be a nation where all men and women are welcome, regardless of race or creed. Thank you for blessing us with freedom and liberty to serve you. Thank you for blessing us with prosperity so that we are a blessing to other nations.

We pray now for your continued blessing and protection upon America. We ask you to endow our leaders with wisdom and understanding that comes from above to lead our country in a way that is pleasing to you. Remind our leaders that you appointed them to their office, and they have a responsibility to serve you and the people.

Lord, take away the greed that is permeating in our hearts, especially in our corporate board rooms. Help us to walk in truth and integrity. We ask that you stay the hand of the enemy that seeks to destroy us. Protect us from ourselves when we become haughty and arrogant. Keep us from destroying ourselves from within. Give us a humble heart and a desire to pray to you seeking your face and turning from our wicked ways so that you will forgive us our sins and heal our land.

We need you Lord. We confess that we have strayed far from you and have served other gods. Turn us back to you. Forgive us and heal our land. Keep your protective hand on our country. Give us clean hearts. Renew a steadfast spirit in us. Do not cast us away from your presence and do not take your Holy Spirit from us. We pray this prayer in the name of your son, Jesus Christ. Amen.

A Prayer for Our Children and Grandchildren

Lord God, we praise you and bless your holy name. You are our God and we honor you with all our being. Father, we come lifting up our children and grandchildren to you. We pray first of all for their salvation. Open their hearts to receive the love and forgiveness of Jesus Christ. Fill them with your Holy Spirit to guide and teach them.

We pray that our young ones will come to know you through study and practice of your Word. Give them a desire to pray to you and to listen for your voice. Protect them from the evil one. Guard their minds from negative thoughts and ungodly teachings. In the name of Jesus, we cancel any plan of the enemy for their destruction. Fill them with the knowledge of you and your will for their life. Keep them on the path of righteousness.

Lord, some of them may be struggling in school or having problems with relationships. Help them to develop good study habits, and give them a desire to always do their best, not being ashamed to strive for excellence. May they realize they can do all things through Christ Jesus who strengthens them. We pray they will always make good decisions weighing consequences for their actions.

Give them a healthy respect for authority, submitting to their parents, teachers and other persons in authority. Purify their hearts, and clean up their attitudes and their language. Curb their tongues to speak good things and not to ridicule or belittle anyone. Give them a spirit so sensitive to you they will be repelled by ungodly movies, music, television shows and games that do not glorify you or your people.
(Continued on next page)

A Prayer for Our Children and Grandchildren (cont'd)

Father, we know you have plans to prosper them so we pray your peace and blessings upon their lives. Thank you for our children and grandchildren. They are fearfully and wonderfully made; marvelous are your works. We pray this in the name of your son, Jesus Christ. Amen.

A Prayer for the Harvest

Father God, we come before you in prayer on behalf of the lost of the world. Your Word says that Jesus came to save the lost and that it is your desire that none should perish. As we intercede, we use our faith believing that thousands have the opportunity this day to receive Jesus Christ as their Lord and Savior.

We ask the Lord of the Harvest to send out laborers to bring the good news of the Gospel in such a way the unsaved will hear and understand. We believe that the lost will not be able to resist the drawing of the Holy Spirit, for you bring them to repentance by your goodness and your love.

In the name of Jesus Christ, we bind the spirit of anti-Christ, and cancel out his assignment to keep the people in bondage to his world. Lord, we pray that the unsaved will hear about the saving power of Jesus Christ wherever they are; in their homes, on their jobs, in the shopping malls, in the sports arenas, riding along the highways. We ask that you saturate them with your Word and speak to their hearts.

Father, give us the power of the Holy Spirit to boldly proclaim the message of salvation to our friends, relatives, associates, neighbors and whoever we come in contact with. Thank you for giving us a desire to pray for souls to be saved. In the name of Jesus we pray. Amen.

Confession of the Church

Lord, as your church, we confess that we have fallen short of your glory on earth and need to seek your forgiveness. Your Word says if we confess our sins you are faithful and just to forgive us. We ask you first of all to forgive us for our lack of prayer. We seem to have time for so many things except to pray to you as a corporate body of believers. Forgive us for not praying and seeking your will before making important decisions in the life of the church.

Forgive us for not being the light of the world, for not witnessing for you as you commanded. Forgive us for losing our salt, our flavor. Forgive us for staying inside and caring more for our church buildings then for your people. Forgive us for fighting among ourselves, for not working together for you, for thinking more highly of ourselves then we ought, for caring more for our tradition then for your Word. Forgive us for the envy and jealousy we have toward other churches, for not seeking to break down racial and denominational barriers, for forgetting that we are all one body in Christ.

Forgive us for tolerating sin in our midst, and not taking corrective actions as your Word says. Forgive us for not teaching your people about the keys to the kingdom and the authority of your name. Forgive us for not using the weapons you have given us to fight off the enemy, and to set your people free.

Lord, we repent of our sins and ask your forgiveness. It is our desire to change our ways so that we will be that church without spot or blemish. Remove from us anything that opposes your Spirit. Transform us to a church that is known for its love and is founded on obedience to your Word. Give us a hunger and thirst for you. Convict us to be faithful to your great commission to go and make disciples. Thank you for your forgiveness. In Jesus' name, we pray.

House of Prayer

Lord, you have said that your house shall be called a house of prayer for all nations. We confess that we have fallen short of your expectations of us and we repent of our sin. Forgive us for not making prayer a priority in our lives, and in the life of the church. We ask that you convict us of our prayerlessness and inspire us to become a house of prayer.

Forgive us for our self-centered prayers and hearts that are cold. Give us the compassion of Jesus. Open our eyes to see the fields ripe for harvest. Stir our hearts to intercede for the lost because you want all people to be saved. Remind us to keep praying for your saints who minister in the harvest fields. Help us not to become weary for at the proper time we will reap a harvest if we do not give up.

Lord, grant us perseverance to pray in the Spirit on all occasions with all kinds of prayers and requests. Teach us to pray and depend on you like Jesus did when He walked on earth. Give us a heart for you and a desire to spend time with you, seeking your face and being blessed in your presence.

Lord, we ask that you give us a spirit of wisdom and revelation in the knowledge of You. May the eyes of our understanding be enlightened so we will know the hope of your calling, the riches of the inheritance in the saints? Help us to know the greatness of Your power toward us who believe.

May we walk worthy of you Lord, fully pleasing You, and being fruitful in every good work. May our works be what You want and not want we want to do. Help us to see things from a heavenly perspective where we are now seated with Christ. Be exalted, O Lord, among the people, be exalted in all the earth. Amen.

A Prayer for Our Men

Our Father in heaven, we thank you for the privilege of knowing you as our Father and Creator. You created man in your image and breathe the breath of life in him. You looked on your handiwork and said it was very good!

Father, we come before you to specifically ask for your blessing upon your men. We pray that you will raise strong men who want to have a relationship with you, men who will humble themselves and pray; men who will study your Word and encourage others to study; men who will seek after godliness and holiness in their lives so they can be effective mentors for younger men.

Lord, in the name of Jesus Christ, we come against the enemy who is holding our men in bondage to sin. We rebuke his work and reclaim our men for the kingdom of God. We command every evil spirit to leave right now and be cast into the pit. In the name of Jesus, we loose the power and effects of every deception, device, and influence that satan brings against them.

We ask that your Holy Spirit convict men to the knowledge that you are looking for repentant hearts—hearts that are willing to be melted and molded by you; men who are willing to move out of their comfort zone and take a risk for you. Lord, we pray that you will do a mighty work in their life. Rise up men who are strong but meek and gentle, men who desire knowledge and wisdom and have teachable spirits, and men who know who they are in Christ and will take their stand against the devil.

We thank you Lord for the victory. Thank you for the harvest. Thank you for your love, your mercy, and your forgiveness. In the name of Jesus Christ we pray this prayer. Amen.

Prayer for the Outpouring of the Holy Spirit

Our Father and our God, Holy is your name. Yours, O Lord is the greatness and the power and the majesty and splendor, for everything in heaven and earth is yours. We exalt You as the One who is over all things. We enter into your presence with praise and thanksgiving.

You said in your word that if we would humble ourselves and pray, seek your face, and turn from our wicked ways, you would hear us, forgive our sins and heal our land. We call upon you now to ask for your forgiveness. We repent of our sins. Cleanse our hearts, O Lord. Purge us with hyssop. Give us a broken and a remorseful heart over our sins.

You are our God and we seek your face; our soul thirst for you, our flesh longs for you. As the deer pants for streams of water, so does our soul thirst for you, the Living God. Hear our cry, O God; listen to our prayers. Lead us to the rock that is higher than us.

You said that men ought always to pray and not lose heart. We pray that you will raise prayer warriors who are willing to persevere in prayer for revival and then to sustain it. We pray for a spirit of prayer to ignite in the land until we all become a house of prayer. Help us to lay aside our differences and focus on the things we agree on as we unite in prayer to you for revival.

Lord God, we are praying for an outpouring of your Spirit on the earth today. We are looking for an open heaven over us where your presence is manifested in glory like it did in the *(continued on next page)*

Prayer for the Outpouring of the Holy Spirit, (cont'd)

temple. Descend on us and shake the house as you did with the early church. Revive us according to your word. In the name of Jesus we pray. Amen

1 Chronicles 29:11; 2 Chronicles 7:14; 2 Chronicles 5:14; Psalm 42:1; Psalm 51:7, 17; Psalm 61:1-2; Psalm 63:1; Psalm 100; Matthew 21:13; Luke 18:1; Acts 4:31

Prayer for Our Fathers

Lord, we thank you for our fathers, whether they are biological fathers or spiritual fathers. Thank you for teaching them how to be loving, kind, strong, tender, supportive, and giving.

We speak a blessing on these men for their faithfulness, and dedication to these responsible positions you ordained for them. We speak a blessing upon them because they have worked long and tirelessly to raise their families, and to be good role models for them. While they may not be perfect fathers, they are the ones you gave us and we love them.

We pray that you save those fathers who have not yet given their heart to you. Invade their dreams with visions of Jesus. Give them a mighty visitation from heaven and place them in your kingdom.

Help all of us to understand how you value the role of the father in the home. Turn the heart of the fathers to the children, and the heart of the children to the fathers *(Malachi 4:6)*. Call all the prodigal fathers back to their rightful positions so they can make a difference in the lives of their children.

Lord, thank you for blessing our fathers. We honor them, but most of all we honor you. In Jesus' name, we pray. Amen.

Prayer for Racial Harmony

Father in heaven, we praise and thank you for your wonderful gift of life. We thank you for the beautiful diversity of people, talents and gifts with which you have blessed us in the body of Christ.

We do confess that we have sinned against you in not carrying out your mandate to come together as one body in Jesus Christ. We repent on behalf of our forefathers and ourselves for participating in the sin of prejudice and racism of people of other ethnicity, resulting in a separation in our worship services. Please forgive us for this sin. We now recognize how we have hindered the unity and the true purpose of your church.

May the mind of Jesus Christ truly be in us as we celebrate the diversity in your body in the spirit of harmony and togetherness. We purpose to love and worship together and to be known as your disciples because of our love for each other. We also purpose to utilize your spiritual weapon of forgiveness for any past hurts we may have received by someone of another ethnicity. Lord, bring healing and wholeness to our hearts and to your Church.

In the name of Jesus, we pray. Amen.